THE PUB QUIZ E

Daniel Morehen

CONTENTS

THE PUB QUIZ

The Pub quiz has become an increasingly popular pastime for pub regulars to enjoy and for pub landlords to entice new customers.

When our resident quiz master decided to stop hosting the quiz, the landlord of my local pub proposed two options to the regular attending quiz teams. He was either going to find us a new quiz master or suggested that the teams take it turns to set the quiz each week, with the team that sets the quiz that particular week getting free drinks for the night – this was a no brainer!

The teams duly started to compile our own quizzes.

FORMAT

The format that we have adopted is six rounds of ten questions with a 15 minute break after round three.

A typical quiz for us looks like this,

Round 1 – General Knowledge

Round 2 – Specialist subject, i.e. Geography, Sport, Films, History etc

Round 3 – Connections

Round 4 - Specialist subject, i.e. Geography, Sport, Films, History etc

Round 5 – In the news (our quizzes are held on Sunday nights so these are topical questions about events that occurred during the week)

Round 6 – Music round

The music round doesn't have to be just songs from your favourite playlist. Why not group songs together from a particular year and invite teams to guess this for a bonus point or group songs with a connection in their title for the teams to work out.

Each team can play a joker, whereby their points for that round are doubled. We ask the teams to play the joker before they answer the questions but this is up to you. As long as the rules of playing the joker are set in advance you should have no problems!

All rounds are straight forward ten questions except the connections round. This has nine questions in which the answers all connect a subject matter or a person. Each team has two lives to guess the connection. If a team gets the connection on question one they get nine bonus points, if they get it on question two they get eight bonus points and so on. The answer to question ten is the connection, so there is a possible nineteen points to be gained.

We also typically have two handout picture rounds which can be completed in the interval and collected in at the end of the quiz. One of these can be 10 celebrities for example or another popular theme is "Dingbats" or anagrams.

We swap answer sheets and mark each other's answers at either the end of each round or at the end of round three or six.

PREPARATION

Don't underestimate the time it takes to set a well thought out quiz. Think of what rounds you are going to have well in advance of the actual quiz night itself and rehearse the questions to yourself and preferably someone else who is not attending the quiz.

Double check your answers. Just because you heard an interesting "fact" on the radio or on a TV panel show, it doesn't necessarily mean it's true! – You will have plenty of people questioning your answers with you on the night!

Avoid questions that are too easy – there is no point to them! I've been to quizzes before where nine questions are so obvious and easy the round all hinges on who knows the hard number 10 question. – It's OK for teams to score only 3 or 4.

Don't be too biased towards one team. If you are running the quiz in your local pub there is a good chance you will already know most of the people and their favourite subjects. One of our team works in the motor sport industry and is an expert in Formula one so I tend to avoid questions on this subject.

I know some people like them but I always try to avoid multiple choice questions. There nothing more annoying than being given multiple choice answers to a question you knew the answer to anyway.

Have a couple of tie-breaker questions up your sleeve. You will need these if the scores are level at the end of the quiz.

Prepare plenty of answer sheets and picture round handouts – You can't have two teams sharing!

Bring spare pens and paper.

If you have prepared a music round make sure you have the means of playing the music!

Make sure everyone is aware of the rules & understand how to play their jokers etc.

Have fun and remember – the quizmaster is always right!

GENERAL KNOWLEDGE QUESTIONS

GENERAL KNOWLEDGE 1

Questions

1. Which UK city was the first to introduce a congestion charge?
2. Which is the only UK national park to have a city within its boundaries?
3. What does the word "Para" mean as in Paralympics?
4. Prince Philip was born on which Greek island?
5. In which year was the pound coin introduced?
6. What does the computer acronym USB stand for?
7. What do the two M's represent in the sweets M&M's?
8. At which town did Billy Butlin open his first holiday camp?
9. Who was the first black player to captain the England football team?
10. Which is the smallest member of the flute family?

Answers

1. Durham
2. The Norfolk Broads
3. Beside or Alongside
4. Corfu
5. 1983
6. Universal serial bus
7. Mars & Murrie (Forrest E Mars and Bruce Murrie)
8. Skegness
9. Paul Ince
10. Piccolo

GENERAL KNOWLEDGE 2

Questions

1. Which was the first Carry on film to feature Barbara Windsor?
2. How many feet are there in a fathom?
3. Which London address is the only one with the postcode SW1A 1AA?
4. Which country has the world's oldest flag?
5. How many teats does a cow normally have?
6. What was the roman name for Scotland?
7. How many Englishmen have played James Bond in authorised films?
8. Which premier league football team are nicknamed the Eagles?
9. What is the national bird of India?
10. How many consecutive shots does it take to score a 147 break in a game of Snooker?

Answers

1. Carry on Spying
2. Six
3. Buckingham Palace
4. Denmark
5. Four
6. Caledonia
7. Two – *Roger Moore and Daniel Craig*
8. Crystal Palace
9. Peacock
10. 36

GENERAL KNOWLEDGE 3

Questions

1. Which island country has the highest number of snake bite fatalities each year?
2. What is a female Donkey called?
3. Bagpuss sits in whose shop window?
4. What was Billy the Kid's birth name?
5. At the start of a game of draughts, how many squares are not covered by pieces?
6. How many hearts does an Octopus have?
7. Who was the British prime minister at the outbreak of World war one?
8. What is the main ingredient to Mock turtle soup?
9. Which country is home to the chicken restaurant Nando's?
10. Which was the first James Bond theme to be nominated for an Oscar?

Answers

1. Sri Lanka
2. Jenny
3. Emily's
4. Henry Patrick McCarty
5. 40
6. Three
7. Herbert Asquith
8. Calf's head or Brains
9. South Africa
10. Live and Let Die

GENERAL KNOWLEDGE 4

Questions

1. Which children's character has "terrible tusks and terrible teeth in his terrible jaws"?
2. Which boy band represented the UK at the 2011 Eurovision song contest?
3. Nazi official Klaus Barbie was known as the Butcher of where?
4. Who allegedly said "Come here Watson, I want you" on 10th march 1876?
5. What is the world's smallest flightless bird?
6. In which country are Hyundai cars made?
7. What does a Village have that a Hamlet doesn't?
8. On which island is Mount Etna?
9. Which historical figure was Doncaster airport formally known as?
10. What did Barbie get for the first time in 1962?

Answers

1. The Gruffalo
2. Blue
3. Lyon
4. Alexander Graham Bell
5. Kiwi
6. South Korea
7. A church
8. Sicily
9. Robin Hood
10. A car

GENERAL KNOWLEDGE 5

Questions

1. ASDA is owned by which American retailer?
2. Which member of ABBA is not Swedish?
3. Which Italia football club did Paul Gascoigne play for?
4. What is the name of the sequel to the TV sit com Porridge?
5. In which city did Archduke Ferdinand get assassinated in 1914 resulting in part to World war one?
6. What is the name of the clarified butter used in Indian cookery?
7. Which piece of sports equipment is 5ft 8in above the ground?
8. What colour is the Jubilee line on a London underground map?
9. German car giant BMW has its headquarters in Munich. What does BMW stand for?
10. Name the five characters that appear in the Enid Blyton books "The famous five"?

Answers

1. Wal-Mart
2. Anni-Frid (Frida) *She is Norwegian*
3. Lazio
4. Going Straight
5. Sarajevo
6. Ghee
7. Dartboard
8. Grey
9. Bayerische Motoren Werke (*Bavarian Motor Works*)
10. Julian, Dick, George, Anne and Timmy *(the dog)*

GENERAL KNOWLEDGE 6

Questions

1. Nicolas Breakspear is the only Englishman to hold which title?
2. The Wiki in Wikipedia stems from the Hawaiian word "wiki wiki". What does it mean?
3. Which US president was assassinated on 6th September 1901 in Buffalo, New York?
4. Which two countries were involved in the 1939 "winter war"?
5. What does an Oscar hold in its hands?
6. In which country was the revolutionary Che Guevara born?
7. Which French dish is also a collective noun for clouds?
8. What was the name of the British submarine that sank the Argentine battleship *General Belgrano* during the Falklands war in 1982?
9. Which world famous landmark is found on mount Lee?
10. Which 5 teams did Bryan Clough manage?

Answers

1. The Pope
2. Fast
3. William McKinley
4. Russia and Finland
5. A Sword
6. Argentina
7. Soufflé
8. HMS Conqueror
9. The Hollywood Sign
10. Hartlepool, Derby, Brighton, Leeds and Nottingham Forrest

GENERAL KNOWLEDGE 7

Questions

1. What was the first song to be played on MTV?
2. Winston and Julia lead a doomed romance in which cult novel?
3. Which famous artist's last words were "Where is my clock"?
4. Which French card game did James Bond often play at the Casino?
5. What is the more common name for the Society of Friends?
6. On a London underground map, what colour is the District line?
7. Which British city has the busiest heliport in the UK?
8. At which school were Tom Brown's schooldays actually spent?
9. What was the currency of the Netherlands before the Euro?
10. Which bird was the name of the enemy in the 1960's TV show The Man from uncle?

Answers

1. Video killed the radio star
2. 1984
3. Salvador Dali
4. Baccarat
5. Quakers
6. Green
7. Aberdeen
8. Rugby
9. Guilder
10. Thrush

GENERAL KNOWLEDGE 8

Questions

1. What is the name of the high school that Sandy attends in Grease?
2. What is a collective noun for Butterflies?
3. Until 1980, Annie Lennox and Dave Stewart were members of which band?
4. Which film about playing football for the Hounslow Harriers was the first western made movie to be shown on North Korean television?
5. The Mexican food "Burrito", translated means "little" what?
6. A Dwarf Lantern is the smallest what in the world?
7. RADA is the parliament in which country?
8. Multiple choice – Which of these is a river in central Siberia? Tom, Dick or Harry
9. Douglas Fairbanks was the 1st man to play which foxy character in 1920?
10. Dr Who's time machine is called TARDIS. What do the letters stand for?

Answers

1. Rydell High
2. Kaleidoscope
3. The Tourists
4. Bend it like Beckham
5. Donkey
6. Shark
7. Ukraine
8. Tom
9. Zorro
10. Time and relative dimensions in space

GENERAL KNOWLEDGE 9

Questions

1. In Sherlock Holmes, what is Dr Watson's first name?
2. How many American flags have been planted on the moon?
3. In which religion is Bondye the supreme creator?
4. Which European capital city means "White city" when translated?
5. Who is the oldest player to score a premier league goal?
6. Which company is the largest producer of tyres?
7. Which Mexican food means "Little Donkey"?
8. Which member of NATO has no standing army?
9. According to the makers, what is "crafted with 56 roots, herbs and spices"?
10. What is the northernmost city in the world with a population of more than one million?

Answers

1. John
2. Six
3. Voodoo
4. Belgrade
5. Teddy Sherringham (40 years and 268 days old)
6. Lego
7. Burrito
8. Iceland
9. Jagermeister
10. St Petersburg

GENERAL KNOWLEDGE 10

Questions

1. What was the name given to the world's first cloned cat?
2. What is the collective noun for Elephants?
3. Which weapon is named after Thomas A Swift?
4. What is Hansen's disease better known as?
5. Alliumphobia is the fear of what?
6. According to the Hitchhikers guide to the galaxy, what are the two most intelligent creatures on Earth?
7. What is the ladies equivalent to the Ryder Cup?
8. Named after a Holy Roman Emperor, what was the code name for Nazi Germanys invasion of the Soviet Union?
9. Elton John was born Reginald Kenneth Dwight. What is his middle name today?
10. What is the name of the ancient form of brain surgery that stems from the Greek word for borer or auger?

Answers

1. CC *(Copy cat)*
2. A Parade
3. TASER *(Thomas A Swift electric rifle)*
4. Leprosy
5. Garlic
6. Mice and Dolphins
7. The Solhiem Cup
8. Operation Barbarossa
9. Hercules
10. Trepanning

GENERAL KNOWLEDGE 11

Questions

1. Amos Brearley was the landlord of which fictional pub from 1948 to 1991?
2. The extinct Dodo bird was native to which island?
3. A Descent is the collective noun for which animal?
4. What was Nazi Germanys codename for the invasion of Britain?
5. What US City was nicknamed "Hitsville USA"?
6. What does an "OOZIE" do for a living in Myanmar (Burma)?
7. What was the code name given to the first detonation of a nuclear weapon?
8. Which two bands had six or more number one hit singles in the UK charts during the 1970s?
9. Which is the only football club to have won the championship in all 4 divisions and the FA cup at the old and new Wembley?
10. Which island country is the most westerly part of Africa?

Answers

1. The Woolpack
2. Mauritius
3. Woodpecker
4. Sea lion
5. Detroit (Mow town)
6. Trains or rides Elephants
7. Trinity
8. Abba (7) and Slade (6)
9. Portsmouth
10. Cape Verde

GENERAL KNOWLEDGE 12

Questions

1. What was the title of Madonna's controversial 1992 coffee table book?
2. With eight words, what is the longest James Bond theme song title?
3. Who is the 1st female artist to top the UK singles charts as a solo artist, part of a duo, a quartet and a quintet?
4. George W Bush was awarded the Golden Raspberry for worst actor in 2004. Which President has been awarded the Golden Raspberry for worst supporting actor?
5. Eleven of the fifteen most liked tweets ever on Twitter are from the same person. Name the person?
6. Whose motto is "By strength and Guile"?
7. Georgetown is the capital city of which South American country?
8. The ancient Latin female name "Helvetia" appears on all the postage stamps and coins of which European country?
9. How many stories high was each world trade centre tower?
10. Code Red, Michelangelo and Cornficker are all famous examples of what?

Answers

1. Sex
2. We have all the time in the world *(Louis Armstrong)*
3. Melanie C
4. Donald Trump *(Ghosts can't do it. 1990)*
5. Barrack Obama
6. The SBS *(Special Boat Service)*
7. Guyana
8. Switzerland
9. 110
10. Computer Viruses

GENERAL KNOWLEDGE 13

Questions

1. What type of ground seeds are used to make the paste "Tahini"?
2. Zakumi, Striker, Zabivaka and Naranjito are all examples of what?
3. In 1980, which county became the first to elect a woman as president?
4. The Baht is which countries currency?
5. In the tour de France, what is the "Lanterne Rouge"?
6. Who was the Argentinean president during the Falklands War?
7. Hollywood is the nickname given to the Indian film industry. The film industry of which country is known as Lollywood?
8. What name is given to the fruit of a blackthorn?
9. Which country withdrew from NATO in 1966 but rejoined in 2009?
10. In the song "That don't impress me much", what three people doesn't impress Shania Twain?

Answers

1. Sesame Seeds
2. World Cup mascots
3. Iceland
4. Thailand
5. The rider in last place
6. Galtieri
7. Pakistan
8. Sloe
9. France
10. Rocket Scientist, Brad Pitt and Elvis

GENERAL KNOWLEDGE 14

Questions

1. The USA won the IQA World cup in 2018 for a record third time, what does IQA stand for?
2. According to Forbes magazine, who was the highest paid Author in the world in 2017?
3. Which Tennis player was stabbed while player against Magdalena Maleeva in 1993?
4. In Greek Mythology what was Medusa's hair made of?
5. What is a female Swan called?
6. On which island did Napoleon die?
7. Between them the six wives of Henry VIII were of three nationalities – English, Spanish and what?
8. Larks Head, Cat's Paw and Monkeys fist are all examples of what?
9. How many balls are there on the table at the start of a normal game of pool?
10. Woman Hitler is an anagram of which relative?

Answers

1. International Quidditch Association
2. JK Rowling
3. Monica Seles
4. Snakes
5. A Pen
6. St Helena
7. German *(Ann of Cleves)*
8. Knots
9. 16
10. Mother in Law

GENERAL KNOWLEDGE 15

Questions

1. What was the last port of call for the Titanic?
2. What is the name of the contemporary sculpture, designed by Antony Gormley? It was completed in 1998 and is known by some local people as the "Gateshead Flasher"
3. What do the 100 folds in a French Chefs hat represent?
4. For which modern Olympic Games was the torch relay first introduced?
5. Mormons belong to the LDS Church, what does LDS stand for?
6. Which band has released a beer called mmmhop?
7. In which 3 films do Tom Cruise and Nicole Kidman play on screen couples?
8. Which fruit is used to make a Black forest gateau?
9. Who presented the first ever edition of Mastermind?
10. Who were the two original presenters of the Clothes show when it was first broadcast in October 1986?

Answers

1. Cove or Cobh *(Cork Harbour) or Queenstown as it was known back then*
2. The Angel of the North
3. The 100 different ways to cook an egg
4. Berlin 1936
5. Latter day saints
6. Hanson
7. Days of Thunder, Far and Away and Eyes wide shut
8. Cherries
9. Magnus Magnusson
10. Jeff Banks and Selina Scott

GENERAL KNOWLEDGE 16

Questions

1. ADSL is a term associated with the internet – what does ADSL stand for?
2. Suva is the capital city of which island nation?
3. Southend Pier is the longest in Britain, which Pier is the second longest?
4. Tiger Woods has been back in winning ways recently, but what is Tigers real first name?
5. Who does Adrian Mole lust after?
6. With which country does Russia share its shortest border (19km)?
7. Who said "there are known known's; there are things we know we know. We also know there are known unknowns; that is to say we know there are some things we do not know. But there are also unknown unknowns – the ones we don't know we don't know"?
8. Which film begins with the words "I'm going back to Australia"?
9. Dick Grayson is better known as whom?
10. The Battle of Coronel, was a naval battle in World War 1 off the coast of which country?

Answers

1. Asymmetric digital subscriber line
2. Fiji
3. Southport
4. Eldrick
5. Pandora
6. North Korea
7. Donald Rumsfeld
8. Grease
9. Robin *(Batman)*
10. Chile

GENERAL KNOWLEDGE 17

Questions

1. A Bitcoin was used for the first time in a commercial transaction in 2010 to buy what?
2. In which capital city were the 1940 Olympic games supposed to of been held?
3. A skyscraper is defined as a building 150metres tall. Which two cities in the world have more than 250 Skyscrapers?
4. In which country was the Orange revolution in 2004?
5. Homey Airport, which is its correct name, is more commonly known as what?
6. Which song topped the UK singles chart in 2018, only to plummet to number 97 one week later? (Furthest one week fall from the top spot in UK chart history)
7. Michael J Fox was born in which country?
8. Angel falls, is the world's highest waterfall. In which country is it located?
9. What was the name of Columbus's ship on his first voyage to the Americas in 1492?
10. What was used for the very first time in the world on 1st January 2002 on the island of La Reunion in the Indian Ocean?

Answers

1. Pizza
2. Tokyo
3. New York and Hong Kong
4. Ukraine
5. Area 51
6. Three Lions
7. Canada
8. Venezuela
9. Santa Maria
10. Euros

GENERAL KNOWLEDGE 18

Questions

1. Who was the last person to win a Grand slam tennis singles final with a wooden racquet?
2. Officially opened in October 2018. The statue of unity is the world's tallest statue. In which country is it located?
3. In which communist country did the first McDonalds open in 1988?
4. The Pulitzer Prize is associated with which profession?
5. What is a Badgers home called?
6. Sir Isaac Newton featured on which British banknote?
7. Ian Flemming international airport is in which country?
8. The Manuka tree, from where we get Manuka honey, is native to which country?
9. Julian Assange, the founder of Wiki leaks, was born in which country?
10. Quicksilver was the common name for which metal?

Answers

1. John McEnroe *(1981 US open)*
2. India
3. Yugoslavia
4. Journalism
5. A Sett
6. £1
7. Jamaica
8. New Zealand
9. Australia
10. Mercury

GENERAL KNOWLEDGE 19

Questions

1. What is the boiling point of water in Fahrenheit?
2. Other than the Merchant of Venice which other Shakespeare play is set in Venice?
3. Who did Hitler designate as his successor in the last days of World War 2?
4. Which visible aid was first introduced for the 1933 FA cup final between Everton and Manchester City?
5. What is the opposite of Stockholm syndrome?
6. Which Film is based upon the book "Do androids dream of electric sheep" by Philip Dick?
7. If you are on a boat called "maid of the mist", which natural spectacle are you looking at?
8. Although a founding member of the United Nations, Which island country lost its UN membership in 1971?
9. When women first got the vote in Britain in 1918, how old did they have to be?
10. In the formula E=mc2, what is C?

Answers

1. 212F
2. Othello
3. Karl Donitz
4. Numbers on the back of shirts
5. Lima Syndrome
6. Blade Runner
7. Niagara Falls
8. Taiwan *(or Republic of China)*
9. 30
10. Speed of Light *(299,792,458 m/s)*

GENERAL KNOWLEDGE 20

Questions

1. What is the name of the main arena at the Australian open tennis in Melbourne Park?
2. In which year was the channel tunnel opened?
3. What is the largest island in the Mediterranean?
4. Leeds castle is in which county?
5. King Zog ruled which country?
6. Aleksei Leanox was the first man to do what?
7. Who wears the red polka dot jersey in the Tour de France?
8. Michael Bond created which children's character?
9. What is written at the bottom of an Ouija board?
10. Which character's name in the Jungle book is said to mean "frog"?

Answers

1. Rod Laver Arena
2. 1984
3. Sicily
4. Kent
5. Albania
6. Space walk
7. The best hill climber
8. Paddington Bear
9. Good bye
10. Mowgli

SPECIALIST SUBJECT QUESTIONS

1980's

Questions

1. Which album released in 1985 by a British band became the first million selling CD recording?
2. Which airline made its maiden flight in June 1984?
3. For which country did Celine Dion win the 1988 Eurovision song contest?
4. Which town in California elected Clint Eastwood as mayor in 1986?
5. In 1985 Live aid was held in Wembley stadium, London and which US venue?
6. In which year of the 1980's did the wearing of seatbelts for drivers and front seat passengers become law in the UK?
7. In which year was the first version of Windows, Windows 1.0 launched?
8. The best selling arcade game of all time was released in May 1980, what was it called?
9. Which oil-tanker ran aground in Prince William sound, Alaska in March 1989?
10. Which football stadium suffered a fire in May 1985 killing 56 spectators?

Answers

1. Brothers in Arms by Dire Straits
2. Virgin Atlantic
3. Switzerland
4. Carmel
5. John F Kennedy Stadium, Philadelphia
6. 1983
7. 1985
8. Pac-man
9. Exxon Valdez
10. Valley Parade, Bradford.

AIRLINES

Questions – can you name the nationality of the following Airlines?

1. Aer Lingus
2. Iberia
3. KLM
4. Avianca
5. TAP
6. Gulf Air
7. Middle East Airlines
8. Wizzair
9. Lufthansa
10. El Al

Answers

1. Ireland
2. Spain
3. The Netherlands
4. Columbia
5. Portugal
6. Bahrain
7. Lebanon
8. Hungary
9. Germany
10. Israel

CAPITAL CITIES

Questions – can you name the capital cities of the following countries?

1. Austria
2. Cameroon
3. Oman
4. Serbia
5. Bolivia
6. Croatia
7. Uganda
8. Indonesia
9. Namibia
10. Lithuania

Answers

1. Vienna
2. Yaounde
3. Muscat
4. Belgrade
5. Sucre
6. Zagreb
7. Kampala
8. Jakarta
9. Windhoek
10. Vilnius

CITIES 1

Questions

1. Measured in metres below sea level, which city in the West Bank is the lowest city in the world?
2. With just under 7,000 inhabitants, what is the least populated capital city in the EU?
3. Reykjavik is the most northern capital city in the world, what is the 2nd?
4. What is the capital city of Kazakhstan, which translated literarily means "capital city"?
5. What is England's newest city? (last city to be granted city status)
6. Which city is served by Marco Polo airport?
7. What is the state capital of Ohio?
8. Which US city is home to the 76ers, the eagles and the Flyers?
9. Which Scottish city is known as the "Granite City"?
10. Which four capital cities does the river Danube flow through?

Answers

1. Jericho
2. Valetta, Malta
3. Helsinki, Finland
4. Astana
5. Chelmsford (2012)
6. Venice
7. Columbus
8. Philadelphia
9. Aberdeen
10. Vienna, Bratislava, Budapest and Belgrade

CITIES 2

Questions

1. What is the capital city of Ethiopia?
2. What is the oldest capital city in the world?
3. What is the southernmost capital city in the world?
4. Which US city is nicknamed the "Emerald City"?
5. It is not uncommon for Cities to be divided between states (i.e. Berlin). But what is the only current divided capital city?
6. What is the capital city of Somalia?
7. Louis Armstrong international airport serves which US city?
8. What is the largest city in Africa by population?
9. What is the capital city of Haiti?
10. Which US city is home to the Celtics basketball team?

Answers

1. Addis Ababa
2. Damascus
3. Wellington
4. Seattle
5. Nicosia
6. Mogadishu
7. New Orleans
8. Lagos (Nigeria)
9. Port au Prince
10. Boston

EUROPE

Questions

1. Glam rock band "Europe" had a number one hit with "The Final Countdown". Which country do they originate from?
2. What is the longest river in Germany?
3. Beside the UK, which European country has a Queen as its head of state?
4. Ljubljana is the capital city of which European country?
5. Before adopting the Euro, what was the currency of Austria?
6. Aneto is the highest mountain in which European mountain range?
7. Belgium, France and Germany were three of the six original countries that formed the EU. Name the other three?
8. Christiana is the former name of which European capital city?
9. The European court of human rights is located in which city?
10. How many European countries have a coastline on the Mediterranean Sea?

Answers

1. Sweden
2. Rhine
3. Denmark (Margrethe II)
4. Slovenia
5. Schilling
6. Pyrenees
7. Luxembourg, Italy and The Netherlands
8. Oslo
9. Strasbourg
10. 13 – *Albania, Bosnia, Croatia, Cyprus, France, Greece, Italy, Malta, Monaco, Montenegro, Slovenia, Spain and Turkey*

FILMS 1

Questions

1. In which city is Dirty Harry set?
2. In which film did David Bowie play a prisoner in a Japanese prison camp?
3. In which Bond film does Bond get married?
4. Which film begins with the words "It all began on new year's eve in my thirty second year of being single"?
5. What raced against a Thorndike Special?
6. Who played the headmistress in the film "The belles of St Tinian's"?
7. Who was Nicole Kidman's co-star in the film Moulin Rouge?
8. Who played the president in the film "Air force one"?
9. In which film did Robin Williams play a teacher called John Keating?
10. Which 1980s burnt serial killer was played by Robert Englund?

Answers

1. San Francisco
2. Merry Christmas, Mr Lawrence
3. On her majesty's secret service
4. Brigit Jones's Diary
5. Herbie
6. Alistair Sim
7. Ewan MacGregor
8. Harrison Ford
9. Dead poets society
10. Freddy Krueger

FILMS 2

Questions

1. Which comedy duo were the stars of the movie "Way out West"?
2. Which actor plays Gregory Underwood in the 1981 Scottish coming of age film Gregory's Girl?
3. Which actor has played in more James Bond Films than any other?
4. In 1988, The Four tops had a hit with "Loco in Acapulco" – which film was it taken from?
5. Flash Thompson is a high school bully who appears in which film series?
6. In the film summer holiday, what was the eventual destination of the Routemaster bus?
7. Which Welshman narrated the 2000 film "The Grinch"
8. In which film would you find bookstore owner William Thacker and Hollywood superstar Anna Scott?
9. Which singer played the Goblin King in the film Labyrinth?
10. What was the name of the robot in the 1986 film "Short Circuit"

Answers

1. Laurel and Hardy
2. Gordon John Sinclair
3. Desmond Llewellyn *(played Q)*
4. Buster
5. Spiderman
6. Athens
7. Anthony Hopkins
8. Notting Hill
9. David Bowie
10. Johnny 5

FILMS 3

Name the film star, who connects each group of films,

1. The Mask, The Cable Guy and Dumb and Dumber
2. Houdini, The Great Race and The Boston Strangler
3. Seven, Meet Joe Black and Thelma and Louise
4. Flat liners, Hook and The Pelican Brief
5. Mermaids, Moonstruck and Tea with Mussolini
6. The Dirty Dozen, Cat Ballou and Gorky Park
7. Little Women, Edward Scissorhands and Beetlejuice
8. Klute, The China Syndrome and Coming Home
9. Speed, Chain Reaction and Dracula
10. All about Eve, The Little Foxes and Whatever happened to Baby Jane

Answers

1. Jim Carey
2. Tony Curtis
3. Brad Pitt
4. Julia Roberts
5. Cher
6. Lee Marvin
7. Winona Ryder
8. Jane Fonda
9. Keanu Reeves
10. Bette Davies

FILMS 4

Questions

1. Who drives a Ford V8 Interceptor, known as the "Pursuit Special"?
2. In which film does "The Bridge of Death" span the "Gorge of eternal peril"?
3. Ernst Stavro Blofeld is the leader of which criminal organisation?
4. In the film Rainman, Dustin Hoffman says he would be willing to fly on only one airline because of its safety record, what was the airline?
5. What was the name of the 2002 film starring Jenifer Lopez as a hotel room attendant who falls in love with a high profile politician?
6. Who is the Neighbour in Toy Story that all of Andy's toys fear?
7. Which animal does Indiana Jones hate?
8. Who played Fred Flintstone in the 1994 film "The Flintstones?
9. What was the name of the 1999 horror film that tells the story of three student filmmakers who go missing in the woods whilst producing a documentary about a local legend?
10. Who played the lead roles in Bill & Ted's excellent adventure?

Answers

1. Mad Max
2. Monty Python and the Holy Grail
3. SPECTRE
4. Qantas
5. Maid in Manhattan
6. Sid Philips
7. Snakes
8. John Goodman
9. Blair witch project
10. Keanu Reeves and Alex Winter

FOOD AND DRINK 1

Questions

1. Which vegetables, popular in Chinese dishes, are the bulb like stems of the Bulrush?
2. Which spirits name derives from a Dutch word that means "Burnt Wine"? *Brandy*
3. Which monk invented sparkling wine?
4. What is the name of the Turkish dish of vine leaves stuffed with rice, chopped meat and onions?
5. What is the traditional thanksgiving desert served in the United States called?
6. What does CAMRA stand for?
7. What are devils on horseback
8. Which pasta translated means "little tongues"?
9. What meat is used in a Glamorgan Sausage?
10. What is the name of a very popular edible product that translated means "twice cooked"

Answers

1. Water Chestnut
2. Brandy
3. Dom Perignon
4. Dolmas
5. Pumpkin Pie
6. Campaign for real ale
7. Prunes wrapped in bacon
8. Linguine
9. None – its vegetarian
10. Biscuit

FOOD AND DRINK 2

Questions

1. The name for which Indian curry dish translated means "hot fry"?
2. The name of which stew stems from the French word for "to revive the taste"?
3. What is the name of the cocktail with equal parts champagne and orange juice? (one word)
4. Although many think of it as a vegetable, which fruit is the main ingredient in the eastern Mediterranean dish "baba ghanoush"?
5. In the Persian language the word for which snack translated means "Elephant farts"?
6. What is the name of the Swedish fermented Herring dish which is said to be the world's smelliest food?
7. What does Basmati mean?
8. What two kinds of Fish are in a Nicoise Salad?
9. What kind of meat is used in the Italian dish "Osso Bucco"?
10. What is the fried dish of leftover cooked potatoes and cabbage called?

Answers

1. Jalfrezi
2. Ragout
3. Mimosa *(Not Bucks Fizz which is 2 parts Champagne to 1 part orange)*
4. Aubergine
5. Pop Corn
6. Surstromming
7. Fragrant or Aromatic
8. Tuna and Anchovy
9. Veal
10. Bubble and Squeak

FOOD AND DRINK 3

Questions

1. What kind of loaf is literally "Toni's bread"?
2. Which is the only vegetable that is also a flower?
3. Black Krim, Green Zebra and Yellow Pear are all varieties of what?
4. Lyonnaise potatoes are Potatoes cooked with what?
5. What cocktail consists of Tia Maria, Vodka and coke?
6. What is the German word for store?
7. From what fish does Caviar come?
8. What do the initials UHT refer to in relation to milk?
9. Vermicelli translated literally means what?
10. From which fruit is Grenadine obtained?

Answers

1. Panatone
2. Broccoli
3. Tomatoes
4. Onions
5. Black Russian
6. Lager
7. Sturgeon
8. Ultra heat treated
9. Little worms
10. Pomegranate

FOOD AND DRINK 4

Questions

1. What is a Bianca Pizza?
2. What are the 5 spices in Chinese Five Spice?
3. What type of food is Cornish Yarg?
4. In the US it is known as Cilantro – What do we call it?
5. Which fish gives Worcestershire sauce its distinctive flavour?
6. What type of pasta translated means little worms?
7. What is the scale called that is used to measure the heat of chillies?
8. Hawke's Bay is a wine making region in which country?
9. In Japanese cooking what is Nori?
10. What would you find inside a baked Alaska?

Answers

1. Pizza without any topping
2. Cinnamon, Cloves, Fennel, Star anise and Szechwan peppercorns
3. Cheese *(covered in nettles)*
4. Coriander
5. Anchovy
6. Vermicelli
7. Scoville
8. New Zealand
9. Seaweed
10. Ice Cream

FOOD AND DRINK 5

Questions

1. What is the name of the German dish of fermented cabbage called"?
2. What did John Pemberton invent in 1886?
3. In which country is Tabasco sauce made?
4. What is an Irish Peach?
5. What is made at St James's Gate in Dublin?
6. What are the two main ingredients of a Hollandaise sauce?
7. Which tyre manufacturer has been giving restaurants stars since 1900?
8. What is the main ingredient of Tapenade?
9. What is Laver bread made from?
10. What drink comprises Rum, Coconut milk and pineapple?

Answers

1. Sauerkraut
2. Coca-cola
3. USA
4. Apple
5. Guinness
6. Egg yolks and butter
7. Michelin
8. Olives
9. Seaweed
10. Pina Collada

FOOD AND DRINK 6

Questions

1. Pecorino cheese is made from the milk of which animal?
2. What type of pulses is used in hummus?
3. What is the fruit flavour in Cointreau?
4. What type of bean is used in Baked Beans?
5. Guinness is brewed in Dublin, But in which Irish city is Murphy's brewed in?
6. Wiener schnitzel, a national dish of Austria, is what type of meat?
7. Which cocktail consists of Vodka, Tia Maria and coke?
8. If you ordered Coquille St Jacques in France, which shellfish would you be ordering?
9. Which fish is the traditional ingredient of the Scandinavian dish Gravad Lax?
10. If you ordered a Bhindi Bhaji in an Indian restaurant what stuffed vegetable would you be ordering?

Answers

1. Sheep
2. Chick Peas
3. Orange
4. Haricot
5. Cork
6. Veal
7. Black Russian
8. Scallops
9. Salmon
10. Okra

FORMER CURRENCIES

Questions – can you name the currencies of the following countries before adopting the Euro?

1. Austria
2. Cyprus
3. Estonia
4. Finland
5. Greece
6. Malta
7. Netherlands
8. Portugal
9. Slovakia
10. Slovenia

Answers

1. Schilling
2. Pound
3. Kroon
4. Markka
5. Drachma
6. Lira
7. Guilder
8. Escudo
9. Koruna
10. Tolar

FORMER NAMES

Questions – can you identify the current names of countries and cities from their former names?

1. Siam
2. Formosa
3. Numidia
4. Mesopotamia
5. Kampuchea
6. Petrograd
7. Byzantium
8. Peking
9. Angora
10. Christiana

Answers

1. Thailand
2. Taiwan
3. Algeria
4. Iraq
5. Cambodia
6. St Petersburg
7. Istanbul
8. Beijing
9. Ankara
10. Osla

GEOGRAPHY 1

Questions

1. Montreal is the largest city in which Canadian province?
2. Which country was formerly known as French Sudan?
3. In which country is the Skeleton coast located?
4. How many US states have the word "new" in their name?
5. What is Britain's smallest city?
6. Paphos is an ancient city on which Mediterranean island?
7. What is the capital city of Venezuela?
8. On the north shore of which country would you find the bay of plenty?
9. Beirut is the capital city of which country?
10. Which cities name when translated from Spanish means "The Meadows"?

Answers

1. Quebec
2. Mali
3. Namibia
4. Four – *New Hampshire, New Jersey, New Mexico and New York.*
5. St David's in Pembrokeshire
6. Cyprus
7. Caracas
8. New Zealand
9. Lebanon
10. Las Vegas

GEOGRAPHY 2

Questions

1. Which country became the second communist state in 1924?
2. Name the only democratic country in the world to have the Communist party elected as its government?
3. In which city harbour was the Greenpeace ship The Rainbow Warrior sunk by the French secret service?
4. Hans Adam II is the monarch of which country?
5. George Bush Intercontinental airport serves which US city?
6. Which Australian state capital lies on the Swan River?
7. What is the capital city of Angola?
8. Plymouth was the capital city of which Caribbean island before being completely destroyed or covered in ash and mud when the islands volcano erupted in 1995?
9. Leonardo da Vinci's "The last supper" is found in a convent in which city?
10. Five countries border the Caspian Sea. Russia is one of them; can you name the other four?

Answers

1. Mongolia
2. Nepal
3. Auckland
4. Lichtenstein
5. Houston
6. Perth
7. Luanda
8. Montserrat
9. Milan
10. Turkmenistan, Azerbaijan, Iran and Kazakhstan

GEOGRAPHY 3

Questions

1. El Capitan is a popular rock formation for climbers in which US national park?
2. Which city was the capital of West Germany from 1949 to 1990?
3. What are the only two countries in South America that do not border Brazil?
4. The Palk straight separates which two Asian countries?
5. The original metre was defined as one 10 millionth of the distance from where to where?
6. Which group of islands is closest to the UK but part of Denmark, has a population of 50,000 and its capital city is Torshavn?
7. Which two countries are within the Chernobyl Nuclear disaster exclusion zone?
8. Which capital city was previously known as Salisbury?
9. Ronald Reagan airport serves which Metropolitan area?
10. What is the capital city of Saudi Arabia?

Answers

1. Yosemite
2. Bonn
3. Chile and Ecuador
4. India and Sri Lanka
5. Equator to the North Pole
6. Faroe Islands
7. Belarus and Ukraine
8. Harare
9. Washington
10. Riyadh

GEOGRAPHY 3

Questions

1. Apart from Water, what runs through the mouth of the Amazon River?
2. 16 countries border China, with which country does China share its shortest border?
3. Canada has the longest coastline in the world with just over 200,000kms. Which country has the second longest coastline?
4. Which US state has the Union jack on its flag?
5. Which river flows through the Grand Canyon?
6. What is London's largest park?
7. What is the capital of Tasmania?
8. Seattle is the largest city in which US state?
9. Which is the highest capital city in the world?
10. Can you name 4 countries that the Greenwich meridian passes through?

Answers

1. The Equator
2. Afghanistan
3. Norway
4. Hawaii
5. Colorado
6. Hyde Park
7. Hobart
8. Washington
9. La Paz *(Bolivia)*
10. 4 from UK, France, Spain, Algeria, Mali, Burkina Faso, Togo, Ghana.

HISTORY 1

Questions

1. Which American Battle is sometimes referred to as "Custer's last stand"?
2. What took place on 8th August 1963 at Cheddington in Buckinghamshire?
3. Constance Markievicz was the first woman to be elected to the House of Commons. Which political party was she a member of?
4. Which two men were awarded the Nobel peace prize in 1993?
5. Portuguese East Africa is the former name of which country?
6. The Dickin Medal, bearing the words "We also serve" is awarded to which members of the armed forces?
7. Who was the only Roman Catholic president of the United States?
8. Who first sailed around the Cape of Good Hope?
9. Seeking refuge after the Battle of the River plate, which port and capital city, was the German Battleship "The Admiral Graf Spee" scuttled by its crew?
10. Why was Louise Brown famous in 1978?

Answers

1. Battle of little Bighorn
2. The great train robbery
3. Sinn Fein in 1918
4. Nelson Mandela and FW De Klerk
5. Mozambique
6. Animals
7. John F Kennedy
8. Bartholomeu Dias
9. Montevideo
10. She was the first test tube baby

HISTORY 2

Questions

1. In what year was the Magna Carta first created?
2. According to popular belief, Victoria Cross medals are made from cannons captured during which battle?
3. In 1980, the SAS stormed which Embassy in London after gunmen seized 26 hostages?
4. Discovered by a French solider during a Napoleonic campaign in Egypt in 1799 but surrendered to the British in 1801, what is the name of the stone that is said to have been the key to translating the ancient Hieroglyphic language?
5. Who did Vietnam gain independence from in 1954?
6. Who was the president of Argentina during the Falklands war?
7. Which island did Turkey invade in 1974?
8. Off the coast of which country was the battle of Trafalgar?
9. Who was the first man to fly the Atlantic solo?
10. In which decade did the city of Constantinople become Istanbul?

Answers

1. 1215
2. Siege of Sevastopol
3. Iranian
4. Rosetta Stone
5. France
6. Galtieri
7. Cyprus
8. Spain
9. Charles Lindberg
10. 1930's

IRELAND (The Isle of Ireland)

Questions

1. What is the most common surname in Ireland?
2. The largest freshwater lake in the British Isles is located in Northern Ireland, What is it called?
3. What is the name of the female GAA sport, which is almost identical to the men's sport of Hurling?
4. Which animal did St Patrick banish from Ireland? Chasing them into the sea after they had attacked him.
5. What is the longest river in Ireland?
6. What date is St Patricks Day?
7. Colcannon is the Irish dish of mashed potatoes and what other vegetable?
8. Mary Robinson was the first female president of Ireland, who was the second? –
9. Which Irish author wrote "Gulliver's Travels" in 1726?
10. There are 5 cities in the Republic of Ireland – Dublin being one, can you name the other 4?

Answers

1. Murphy
2. Lough Neagh *(or Loch Eachaidh)*
3. Camogie
4. Snakes
5. Shannon
6. 17th March
7. Cabbage
8. Mary McAleese
9. Jonathon Swift
10. Cork, Limerick, Waterford and Galway

LONDON

Questions

1. On a London underground map, which line is coloured pink?
2. How are the Royal Botanical Gardens better known?
3. What is London's largest meat market?
4. What football club is the oldest in London?
5. What is unique about the public road that leads up to the Savoy hotel?
6. What percentage on the London underground is actually underground?
7. What is the nickname given to the exam London cabbies have to take?
8. What is London's tallest building?
9. What are the names of the three green properties on a Monopoly board?
10. How many London boroughs are there?

Answers

1. Hammersmith and City
2. Kew Gardens
3. Smithfield
4. Fulham
5. You drive on the right hand side of the road
6. 45%
7. The Knowledge
8. The Shard
9. Regent Street, Oxford Street and Bond Street
10. 32

RETAIL

Questions

1. What was the name of the Toys R us Giraffe Mascot?
2. The online ticket exchange company "Stub Hub" is owned by which Dot Com giant?
3. With 2.3 million employees, which retailer is the largest private employer in the world?
4. Smithfield market in London is a place you go to buy what?
5. In 2004 Safeway's was acquired by which rival supermarket chain for £3.3 billion?
6. Which chain sold the most cups of coffee in the UK last year?
7. The Catalogue retailer ARGOS was formed from which British sales promotion scheme?
8. Which retailer is never knowingly undersold?
9. Jack Cohen founded which British retail giant in 1919?
10. What is the full name of the online retailer ASOS?

Answers

1. Geoffrey
2. Ebay
3. Wal-Mart
4. Meat & Poultry
5. Morrison's
6. Costa
7. Green Shield Stamps
8. John Lewis
9. Tesco
10. As seen on screen

SCIENCE AND NATURE

Questions

1. An intrusion is the collective noun for which group of insects?
2. What descriptive term is applied to force 11 on the Beaufort scale?
3. Which temperature has the same value in both centigrade and Fahrenheit?
4. Which element was originally called Hydragyrum?
5. What is an Otters home called?
6. What are Egyptian Mau's, Ragamuffins and Turkish Vans?
7. Which tree do we get turpentine from?
8. A Californian Sheep head is a type of what?
9. How many bones are there in a human hand?
10. Which 2 Planets in the solar system have no moons?

Answers

11. Cockroaches
12. Violent storm
13. -40
14. Mercury
15. Holt
16. Breeds of cat
17. Pine
18. Fish
19. 27
20. Mercury and Venus

SCIENCE FICTION

Questions

1. In the book "The war of the worlds" by HG Wells, where do the Martians first land?
2. Taylor, Landon and Dodge are astronauts in deep hibernation when their spaceship "Liberty 1" crash lands on an unknown planet in which film?
3. Which 1976 film is set in a domed city where to keep the equilibrium of population and consumption of resources, everyone who reaches the age of 30 is killed. People who try to escape the city are called "runners" whilst the police trying the catch the runners are called sandmen?
4. Durran Durran got its name from a Scientist in which Science Fiction film?
5. What was the name of the submarine in Jules Verne's, Twenty thousand leagues under the sea?
6. The 2006 film, Alien Autopsy starred which British comedy Duo?
7. Which film has robots called MAXIMILIAN, VINCENT and BOB?
8. What kills the Aliens in MARS ATTACKS!
9. Which Science fiction franchise is recognised by Guinness world records as the longest running movie franchise having been in on-going production since 1954? To date there have been

33 movies, along with numerous TV programmes, books and video games.

10. Which 1970s TV show "leads a ragtag fugitive fleet on a lonely quest, a shining planet know as Earth"?

Answers

1. Woking, Surrey
2. Planet of the apes
3. Logan's Run
4. Barbarella
5. Nautilus
6. Ant & Dec
7. The Black Hole
8. Slim Whitman's "Indian Love Call" *(Country Music)*
9. Godzilla
10. Battlestar Galactica

SPORTS

Questions

1. Who won the first ever FA cup final at Wembley?
2. The Fed cup is an international team competition in which sport?
3. Which long distance runner famously ran bare foot at the 1984 Olympics?
4. Manchester United won the first ever Premier League title. Who were runners up?
5. Which two countries competed in the world's first international cricket match?
6. Who holds the record the most number of Formula one wins?
7. Which team sport is played on the largest pitch?
8. How many players are there in a Curling team?
9. What colour is the number one ball in pool?
10. Who won the Grand National in 1977?

Answers

1. Bolton Wanderers
2. Tennis
3. Zola Budd
4. Aston Villa
5. USA and Canada
6. Michael Schumaker
7. Polo
8. Four
9. Yellow
10. Red Rum

UNITED STATES OF AMERICA

Questions

1. At 82 metres below sea level, where is America's lowest elevation to be found?
2. McCarran international airport serves which US city?
3. How many cents is a Nickel worth?
4. Kodiak Island is in which US state?
5. In an American diner, if you heard the waitress shout "Chicks on a raft", what would she be ordering?
6. In Baseball, which city are the White Sox from?
7. Who was the first president to resign from office?
8. Four states begin with the letter W. Washington is one, name the other three?
9. Which global brand was created by brothers Richard and Maurice in 1940?
10. How many states share a border with another country?

Answers

1. Bedwater Basin in Death Valley national park
2. Las Vegas
3. Five
4. Alaska
5. Eggs on Toast
6. Chicago
7. Richard Nixon
8. West Virginia, Wisconsin and Wyoming
9. McDonalds
10. 17 in total – *13 with Canada (Alaska, Michigan, Maine, Minnesota, Montana, New York, Washington, North Dakota, Ohio, Vermont, New Hampshire, Idaho and Pennsylvania) and 4 with Mexico (California, Arizona, New Mexico and Texas)*

WINTER OLYMPICS

Questions

1. In which area of South Korea were the 2018 Winter Olympics being held?
2. Which two individual sports make up the Nordic combined event?
3. Torvill and dean won gold with a perfect score in 1984. What piece of music did the couple skate to?
4. Great Britain won 4 medals at the 2014 games. In which 3 sports were these achieved?
5. North Korea is sending two athletes to the games, in which sport will they compete?
6. Whilst the top 3 athletes in each sport get a medal, what do the 4th place competitors get awarded?
7. Based on a true story, the 1993 film "Cool Running's" is about a Bobsleigh team from which country?
8. With a total of 329 medals which nation is the most successful country at the winter Olympics?
9. Which city has been awarded the 2022 games and will be the only city to have hosted both the summer and winter Olympics?
10. Prior to the games in 2018, how many countries have previously held the winter Olympics?

Answers

1. Pyeongchang
2. Ski jump and cross country skiing
3. Ravel's "Bolero"
4. Gold for Women's Skeleton, Silver for Men's Curling and Bronze for Women's Curling and Women's Snowboarding
5. Figure Skating
6. An Olympic Diploma
7. Jamaica
8. Norway
9. Beijing
10. 11

CONNECTIONS ROUNDS

One point for each correct answer plus bonus points depending upon when the team gets the connection right – 9 bonus points if connection got on question 1 etc. Question 10 is the connection.

CONNECTIONS 1

Questions

1. What is the name of the cat employed at 10 Downing Street between 1988-2006, who was named after the civil servant in "Yes Minister"?
2. Which Herefordshire market town located on the river Wye is said to be the birthplace of the British tourist industry?
3. Which Irish county is the birthplace of X factor judge, Louis Walsh?
4. Who was the king of Scotland who signed the Edinburgh-Northampton treaty in 1328?
5. What was the occupation of Thomas Farriner, whose premises started the Great fire of London?
6. Who was the England cricket captain who won the Ashes in 2005?
7. Which British supermodel pleaded guilty to assaulting two police officers at Heathrow Airport?
8. What was the Surname of Orville and Wilbur, inventors of the first airplane?

9. Which Italian sports car manufacturer's symbol is a Prancing Horse?

Answers

1. Humphrey (John Humpries)
2. Ross on Wye (Jonathon Ross)
3. Mayo (Simon Mayo)
4. Robert the Bruce (Ken Bruce)
5. Baker (Danny Baker)
6. Michael Vaughan (Johnny Vaughan)
7. Naomi Campbell (Nicky Campbell)
8. Wright (Steve Wright)
9. Ferrari (Nick Ferrari)
10. Radio presenters / DJ's

CONNECTIONS 2

Questions

1. Which charity founded in 1860 by Mary Tealby aims to never turn away an animal in need of help?
2. Name of the cast iron and plate glass structure originally built in Hyde Park to house the Great Exhibition of 1851?
3. What is the nationality of Leicester goalkeeper Casper Schmeical?
4. Which 1990 romantic fantasy film starred Patrick Swayze, Demi Moore and Whoopi Goldberg?
5. What is the name of the Beatles Film released in 1967, about a group of people on a coach trip that featured the song "I am the Walrus"?
6. What is the name of the former Steeplejack turned television presenter, who in 2004 was awarded a MBE and was quoted as saying "I'm looking forward to meeting the queen but I shall probably have to get a new cap"?
7. Who played Buffy Summers in the television series "Buffy the vampire slayer"?
8. Which Jamaican reggae artist is best known for his hits "Oh Carolina", "Boombastic" and "It wasn't me"?

9. What is the name of the 1996 hit single by the fun loving criminals, which contains samples from the films "Reservoir dogs" and "Pulp Fiction"?

Answers

1. Battersea dogs home
2. Crystal Palace (Crystal cove)
3. Danish (Great Dane)
4. Ghost
5. Magical Mystery Tour (Mystery Machine)
6. Fred Dibnah
7. Sarah Michelle Gellar
8. Shaggy
9. Scooby Snacks
10. Scooby Doo

CONNECTIONS 3

Questions

1. Pteronophobia is the fear of what?
2. On 2nd April 1977, 21 year old Charlotte Brew became the first female what?
3. Which animal is at the centre of festival of "Sanfermines" held in July in Pamplona, Spain?
4. Blue Peter pets Mable, Lucy and Barney are what types of animal?
5. What is the county town of Hampshire, This historic city called "Venta Belgarum" by the Romans?
6. Born in 1983, which long distance runner is the most decorated athlete in British athletics history?
7. Merino, Cashmere and Angora are all types of what?
8. Which Football team became the first premier league champions to be relegated to the third tier of English football in May 2017?
9. Which state in Australia do you find the cities of Ballarat, Geelong and Melbourne?

Answers

1. Feathers (Royal Family)
2. Female Jockey to ride in Grand National (Shameless)
3. The Bull (The Archers)
4. Dog (Hollyoaks)
5. Winchester (Minder)
6. Mo Farah (The Simpsons)
7. Wool (Emerdale)
8. Blackburn Rovers (Coronation Street)
9. Victoria (Eastenders)
10. Fictional Pubs on TV/Radio programmes

CONNECTIONS 4

Questions

1. Which American old west lawman became famous for the capture and then the killing of Billy the kid?
2. What is the name of the character played by Bill Nighy in the 2016 war comedy film whose tagline is "The British Empire Strikes back"?
3. Where is the home to the only wild monkey population in Europe, This peninsula was one of the Pillars of Hercules and was known to the Romans as Mons Calpe?
4. Which American Artist, who was a leading figure in the visual art movement known as "pop art" with works including "Campbell's soup cans" and "The shot Marilyns"?
5. What was the 1980's TV Game show that had the catchphrase "Stay out of the black and into the red, nothing in this game for two in a bed"?
6. Which 1970's rock band had number one hits with "Hot Love", "Telegram Sam" and "Metal Guru"?
7. In the popular nursery rhyme, who has lost her sheep and doesn't know where to find them?
8. Which "The Voice" judge came to fame in 2010 with hit singles "Do it like a dude" and "price tag"?

9. Which American filmmaker, writer, actor, comedian, playwright and musician born in 1935 as Allan Stewart Konigsberg?

Answers

1. Sheriff Pat Garrett
2. Sergeant Wilson
3. Rock of Gibraltar
4. Andy Warhol
5. Bullseye
6. T-Rex
7. Little Bo Peep
8. Jessie J
9. Woody Allen
10. Toy Story

CONNECTIONS 5

Questions

1. Used as lawn ornaments, which diminutive spirit in renaissance magic is said to be a small humanoid that lives underground?
2. Which American Artist, who was a leading figure in the visual art movement known as "pop art" has works including "Campbell's soup cans" and "The shot Marilyn's"?
3. Which governor of the Roman province of Judaea, presided at the trial of Jesus and sentenced him to be crucified?
4. Name the British member of the 1960's TV band "the Monkees"?
5. Who won Wimbledon in 1975, defeating the overwhelming favourite and defending champion, Jimmy Connors?
6. What phrase refers to the supposed phenomenon of novices experiencing a disproportionate frequency of success?
7. With a population of around 1.4 billion, which is the world's most populous country?
8. Which British charity, was launched in 2007 to help provide better facilities for British servicemen and women who have been wounded or injured in the line of duty?

9. Which character was voiced by Robin Williams in the 1992 Disney film Aladdin?

Answers

1. Gnome (The laughing gnome as a Bowie song)
2. Andy Warhol (Bowie played Andy Warhol in the film Basquait)
3. Pontius Pilate (Bowie played Pilate in the film Last temptation of Christ)
4. David Jones (Jones in Bowies real name)
5. Arthur Ashe
6. Beginners Luck
7. China
8. Help for Heroes
9. Genie
10. David Bowie

CONNECTIONS 6

Questions

1. Born in Poland in 1886, who was the primary founder of the state of Israel, and in 1949 was elected as Israel's first prime minister?
2. Which famous person in history had a horse called Marengo?
3. Which woman, dedicated to the relief of the poor, won the Nobel peace prize in 1979 and died in Calcutta in 1997?
4. Who is the famous son of the Greek princess Olympias? He was born in 356BC and is widely considered one of history's most successful military commanders?
5. About which composer was the 1984 film Amadeus?
6. Which former leader of the Solidarity movement, sent his wife to Oslo in 1983 to accept his Nobel peace prize, because he feared that if he went he would not be readmitted to his homeland?
7. Which French leader said "Belgium is a country invented by the British to annoy the French"
8. In 1974, which footballer was accused of stealing a passport and a fur coat from Miss World?
9. Who defeated Richard Nixon to become US president in 1960?

Answers

1. David Ben Gurion (Tel Aviv in Israel)
2. Napoleon Bonaparte (Ajaccio in Corsica)
3. Mother Theresa (Tirana in Albania)
4. Alexander the Great (Skopje in Macedonia)
5. Wolfgang Amadeus Mozart (Salzburg in Austria)
6. Lech Walesa (Gdansk in Poland)
7. Charles De Gaulle (Paris in France)
8. George Best (Belfast in Northern Ireland)
9. John F Kennedy (New York in USA)
10. All had airports named after them

CONNECTIONS 7

Questions

1. What was the name of Lord Nelson's mistress?
2. Which comedian, actress and screenwriter first appeared on TV screens in the 1970's. She was a contestant on the TV talent show New Faces and appeared as a Novelty act on Esther Rantzen's "That's Life". Her most famous comic song is the Ballad of Barry and Freda?
3. What is the name of the American film director, who is frequently cited as one of the greatest and influential directors in cinematic history? He was born in 1928 and died in 1999. His works include Spartacus and 2001: A space Odyssey
4. Who am I? I am a Former Roman solider of Greek origin; I was executed for failing to recant my Christian faith. I am the patron saint of many places including Portugal, Romania, Malta and Catalonia.
5. Also known as the sun root or earth apple, which species of sunflower native to north eastern America is cultivated for its tuber, which is used a root vegetable?
6. In cookery, the term devilled, generally means coated with which powder?
7. What is the opposite of the Stockholm syndrome?

8. What is the name of the tan coloured document holders that are used in offices for the distribution of internal mail which are reused many times?
9. What is the name given to the dish of chicken fillet pounded and rolled around garlic butter, then coated with eggs and bread crumbs and either fried or baked?

Answers

1. Emma Hamilton (Bermuda)
2. Victoria Wood (Seychelles)
3. Stanley Kubrick (Falkland Islands)
4. Saint George (Grenada)
5. Jerusalem Artichoke (Israel)
6. Cayenne Pepper (French Guiana)
7. Lima Syndrome (Peru)
8. Manila Envelopes (Philippines)
9. Chicken Kiev (Ukraine)
10. Capital Cities

CONNECTIONS 8

Questions

1. In 1987, Unemployed antique dealer Michael Ryan fatally shot 16 people before taking his own life in which historic market town?
2. Where is the venue for the annual Henry Wood Promenade concert?
3. Which UNESCO world heritage site which was founded in 1840, it has an area of 300 acres and is home to more than 30,000 kinds of living plants?
4. Which car manufacturer has had models called the Tigra, Magnum and Belmont?
5. What is the capital city of Jamaica.?
6. The Kray twins were among the last people to be held at which former prison?
7. Which battle was fought on 18th June 1815?
8. What was the name of the computer bug that was supposed to result in computer crashes, meltdowns and generally the end of world, at midnight on New Year's Eve 1999?
9. In the nursery rhyme, what is falling down, with attempts in subsequent verses to repair it?

Answers

1. Hungerford
2. Royal Albert Hall
3. Kew Gardens
4. Vauxhall
5. Kingston
6. Tower of London
7. Waterloo
8. Millennium bug
9. London Bridge
10. Thames river bridges in London

CONNECTIONS 9

Questions

1. Which Actor, born in New York in 1899 and died in 1986. He was described by Orson Wells as the greatest actor who ever appeared in front of a camera" – He was nominated for best actor in the films "Yankee doodle dandy, love me or leave me and Angles with dirty faces"?

2. The poor fellow-soldiers of Christ and of the temple of Solomon were a catholic military order formed in 1119 for the protection of Christian pilgrims. They fought many battles against Muslim caphiliates in the holy land. How are they better known?

3. Similar to a Dingbat or a Catchphrase, what is the name of the puzzle which combines illustrated pictures with individual letters to depict words or phrases?

4. Which actress has played roles in the films Armageddon, The incredible hulk and the lord of rings trilogy? She is also the daughter of a famous rock musician

5. Who am I? – I was born in Jamaica in 1958 but represented England at international level, scoring a hatrick on my debut in a 9-0 win against

Luxembourg becoming the 1st black player ever to score a hatrick for England.

6. What is someone who makes arrows called?
7. What is the largest and former capital city of Sri Lanka?
8. What is a 1.5L bottle of wine called?
9. Which TV Presenter and journalist, who was one of original presenters on TV AM, famously extracted an apology from Richard Nixon over the Watergate scandal?

Answers

1. James Cagney (Cagney and Lacey)
2. The Knights Templar (Simon Templar)
3. Rebus
4. Liv Tyler (Sam Tyler – Life on Mars)
5. Luther Blissett
6. Fletcher (Jessica Fletcher)
7. Columbo
8. Magnum
9. David Frost
10. TV Detectives

CONNECTIONS 10

Questions

1. What is the name of the character in Pulp fiction played by Harvey Keitel, who now appears in adverts selling insurance policies?
2. Who am I? I was born in 1943 in Pittsburgh, I am a singer songwriter, I have released 36 studio albums, I have released 50 singles including "Give me the night" and "in your eyes"
3. Katherine Lucy Mary Worsley is better known by what title?
4. What was the name of the ancient network of trade routes that connected the East to the West? The routes began during the Han dynasty around 220BC
5. What is the term given in ten pin bowling when all the pins have been knocked down with the first ball of a frame?
6. Michael Gough, Michael Caine and Jeremy irons have all played Alfred Pennyworth in the movies, but what is Alfred's occupation?
7. What is the nickname given to the Royal Navy, the oldest of the UKs armed services?
8. What is the name of the property that partners Park Lane on a Monopoly board?

9. The world Snooker championships were sponsored by which Brand form 1976 to 2005?

Answers

1. Winston Wolf
2. George Benson
3. Duchess of Kent
4. Silk road
5. Strike
6. Butler
7. Senior service
8. Mayfair
9. Embassy
10. Cigarette brands

CONNECTIONS 11

Questions

1. Who starred alongside Marlon Brando in the 1976 western "The Missouri Breaks"?
2. Who played Gareth Blackstock in the TV sitcom "Chef"?
3. Who was George W Bush's vice president?
4. Phil Silvers is best known for playing which character in the 1950's?
5. Which Artists works include "Brighton Beach", Stratford Mill" and The Valley Farm"?
6. Leonard Fenton played which Character in Eastenders. He was one of the original characters of the show and appeared in Episode 1 in 1985?
7. Which comedy actress co-starred in "The Kenny Everett Television show, often appearing in nothing more than frilly underwear and high heels?
8. What is the name of the mountain pass that runs alongside the border of Afghanistan and Pakistan?
9. Meaning Mother in Latin, what is the name of the most senior nurse in a hospital?

Answers

1. Jack Nicholson
2. Lenny Henry
3. Dick Cheney
4. Sergeant Ernest Bilko
5. John Constable
6. Doctor Harrold Legg
7. Cleo Rocos
8. Khyber Pass
9. Matron
10. Carry on films

CONNECTIONS 12

Questions

1. Which actress plays Sybill Trelawney in the Harry potter films?
2. Who was the first female president of Ireland?
3. What is the real name of American Wrestler "The Rock"?
4. What is name of the Chef who as head chef of the Castle Hotel in Taunton held a Michelin star. He appeared on the BBCs Ready, Steady, Cook over 200 times and is now the celebrity chef on ITVs this morning?
5. What is the name of the Jewish Canadian folk singer, who died in 2016 aged 82, most known for the song "Hallelujah"?
6. Which British driver won the Formula one world championship in 1996?
7. Who has been caretaker manager of England on two separate occasions? The first was in 1999 when Glen Hoddle was sacked and then again in 2000 following Kevin Keegan's resignation
8. Which comedian, born in 1931 and died in 1993, began his career as a pianist which evolved into comedy when he got laughs by playing wrong notes and complaining to the audience. He made his TV debut on Opportunity knocks in 1967 and

was a prominent comic on British TV for the rest of his life?

9. Which former rugby player is married to Zara Philips?

Answers

1. Emma Thompson
2. Mary Robinson
3. Dwayne Johnson
4. Phil Vickery
5. Leonard Cohen
6. Damon Hill
7. Howard Wilkinson
8. Les Dawson
9. Mike Tindall
10. England Rugby World cup winning side 2003

CONNECTIONS 13

Questions

1. Which English radio presenter, TV personality and Artist, was born in 1955. He has appeared on numerous celebrity reality programmes such as I'm a Celebrity and Big Brother, had a number 1 hit record in 1990 had a pet cockatiel called Magic?
2. What is the name of English Cartoonist, comedian and actor who co-founded the magazine Private eye? He was also a regular as a guest on celebrity panel shows such as Blankety blank, Countdown, Celebrity squares and Through the keyhole.
3. Who played Anthony Royal, in the Royal Family?
4. Which former comedian, writer and actor, who died in 2002, was born in India, with the Christian name Terrance which he always disliked. Although refused by the Church where he is buried, it is said that he wanted his headstone to bear the words "I told you I was ill"?
5. Which controversial singer, songwriter was born Stefani Joanne Angelina Germanotta?
6. Who had hits in the 70's with "Hanging on the telephone", "Call me" and "the tide is high?
7. Which Rastafarian, who is credited with popularising reggae music around the world and served as a symbol of Jamaican culture and

identity, died at the age of 36 of skin cancer in 1981?

8. Which Composer, who was born in Germany in 1770, wrote the opera Fidelio. By the time he died in 1827 he was almost completely deaf?

9. What is the name of Charlie Browns pet?

Answers

1. Timmy Mallet (Famous 5)
2. Willie Rushton (Eastenders)
3. Ralph Little (Muppets)
4. Spike Milligan (Tom & Jerry)
5. Lady Gaga (Lady & The Tramp)
6. Blondie (Hitler's Dog)
7. Bob Marley (Marley and me)
8. Ludwig van Beethoven (Beethoven film)
9. Snoopy
10. Dogs

CONNECTIONS 14

Questions

1. Which English actor, comedian, screenwriter and producer, who was born in 1965 started his career on the puppet show Spitting image and also on the Krypton factor as one of the actors who appeared in the observation rounds. Although a stand up comic, he is best known for playing characters?

2. Which former model and television personality who has also competed in several motor racing events was famous for being the fastest celebrity to go round the top gear track in a reasonably priced car in 2003?

3. Who is the lead singer of welsh band The Sterophonics?

4. Born in Hungary in 1874 as Erik Weisz, what is the stage name of the Magician whose famous tricks included escaping handcuffs and straitjackets whilst suspended upside down in water?

5. What is the name of the international multi-sport event for injured armed services personnel creates by Prince Harry?

6. Which Marvel comic book characters name is Wade Winston Wilson?

7. In American football, what is the nickname given to the franchise from Philadelphia?
8. Which pop duo consisted of David Van Day and Theresa Bazar, their hits include O'Lamour and Give me back my heart?
9. What is the name of the former prison located in San Fransico bay?

Answers

1. Steve Coogan
2. Jodie Kidd
3. Kelly Jones
4. Harry Houdini
5. Invictus
6. Deadpool
7. Eagles
8. Dollar
9. Alcatraz
10. Clint Eastwood

CONNECTIONS 15

Questions

1. Which English writer, Television presenter and comedian who died in 2002 aged 73, hosted BBC's points of view from 1979 to 1986?
2. Which iconic symbol of American independence which was manufactured in England in 1751 is located in Philadelphia? The symbol has appeared on US coins, stamps and is on the current $100 note. There is even a replica at Disney world—
3. The author Roald Dahl was born in Cardiff in 1916, what Nationality was his parents?
4. Who is the Roman god of Desire, love, attraction and affection?
5. Which Cricketer, nicknamed the prince, holds the record for the highest individual score in 1st class cricket, with 501 not out for Warwickshire against Durham?
6. What is an important symbol in Arthurian Literature? Different traditions describe it as a cup, dish or stone with powers that provide happiness or eternal youth.
7. What is the name of the Tribunal that started in 1478 and not totally abolished until 1834. Anyone who was not loyal to the Catholic Church was

considered a Heretic and in some cases sentenced to Death?

8. What is the name of the US politician who served as the Governor of Alaska from 2006 to 2009? She was the Republican party nominee for the Vice President in the 2008 election alongside John McCain and is quoted as saying "The only difference between a Hockey Mum and a Pitbull is lipstick"

9. Which food product was introduced in America in 1937 and was intended to increase the sale of pork shoulder. During World War 2 it became the mainstay of a US soldiers diet?

Answers

1. Barry Took (Took was responsible for forming the Python team)
2. Liberty Bell (Theme tune)
3. Norwegian
4. Cupid (Cupids foot from the painting by Bronzino is used in Monty Python)
5. Brian Lara
6. The Holy Grail
7. The Spanish Inquisition
8. Sarah Palin
9. SPAM
10. Monty Python

MUSIC CONNECTION ROUNDS

MUSIC CONNECTIONS 1

1. GRENADE by Bruno Mars
2. CANNON ball by Damien Rice
3. Eton RIFLES by The Jam
4. Chelsea DAGGER by The Fratelli's
5. Connection is Weapons

MUSIC CONNECTIONS 2

1. CHARLIE BROWN by Coldplay
2. PRINCE CHARMING by Adam and the Ants
3. SCOOBY Snacks by Fun Lovin' Criminals
4. MICKEY by Toni Basel
5. Connection is Cartoon Characters

MUSIC CONNECTIONS 3

1. MIRROR man by The Human League
2. The theme from S-EXPRESS by S-EXPRESS
3. Don't let the SUN go down on me by Elton John
4. TIMES like these by the Foo Fighters
5. Connection is Newspapers

MUSIC CONNECTIONS 4

1. Rotterdam by the Beautiful SOUTH
2. NORTHern Star by Melanie C
3. Deep by EAST 17
4. The king of wishful thinking by Go WEST
5. Connection is Compass Directions

MUSIC CONNECTIONS 5

1. Locked out of Heaven by Bruno MARS
2. VENUS by Bananarama
3. Drops of JUPITER by Train
4. Love Kills by Freddie MERCURY
5. Connection is The Solar System

MUSIC CONNECTIONS 6

1. WEST END Girls by The Pet shop boys
2. CIRCLE of life by Elton John
3. The SHOW must go on by Queen
4. The man who can't be moved by the SCRIPT
5. Connection is The Theatre

MUSIC CONNECTIONS 7

1. Use Somebody by The KINGs of Leon
2. Don't stop by Fleetwood MAC
3. Layla by Derek and the DOMINOS
4. The CHICKEN song by Spitting Image
5. Connection is Fast food chains

MUSIC CONNECTIONS 8

1. The Living years by Mike and the MECHANICS
2. Two Princes by The Spin DOCTORS
3. The Joker by The Steve MILLER band.
4. Top of the World by The CARPENTERS
5. Connection is Occupations

MUSIC CONNECTIONS 9

1. Caravan of love by The House MARTINs
2. Girl from Mars by ASH
3. Sweet CAROLINE by Neil Diamond
4. Every day is like Sunday by MORRISEY
5. Connection is Men Behaving Badly

MUSIC CONNECTIONS 10

1. Englishman in NEW YORK by Sting
2. Walking in MEMPHIS by Marc Cohen
3. Viva LAS VEGAS by Elvis Presley
4. Streets of PHILADELPHIA by Bruce Springsteen
5. Connection is US Cities

TIE BREAKER QUESTIONS

Questions

1. In what year was the ring pull invented?
2. How many original songs were recorded by the Beatles (as a band)?
3. How many years in prison did the 12 members of the Great train robbery gang get between them?
4. How many Kilometres is the Suez Canal
5. As a result of weapons testing, how many nuclear explosions have there been?
6. How long (In Earth years) does it take for Pluto to orbit the sun?
7. The M1 is the lowest numbered motorway in the UK, which is the highest?
8. The Shortest war in history was fought between Britain and Zanzibar in 1896. How long did it last?
9. How many Pigeons have won the Dickin medal?
10. What is the world's most populous landlocked country?
11. William Harrison holds the record for the shortest term of the President of the United States. How long was he in office?
12. The song "What do you want?" by Adam Faith holds the record for the shortest song length for a UK number one single. How short is it?

13. The song "All around the World" by Oasis holds the record for the longest song length for a UK number one single. How long is it?
14. Lake Baikal in Russia is the deepest lake in the world. How deep is it?
15. Elvis Presley holds the record for the most combined weeks at number one in the UK singles chart. How many combined weeks?
16. How many square Kilometres does the Atlantic Ocean occupy?
17. How many people visited Ronald Reagan while he was lying in state?
18. In what year did Joan of Arc die?
19. At the 2018 World cup, Iceland became the smallest nation to play in the finals. What was the population of Iceland at that time?
20. On what date was the first premium bond purchased?
21. How many films did Laurel and Hardy make?
22. How many Victoria crosses were award in World War one?
23. How many countries drive on the left?
24. In which year was Microsoft formed?
25. How many steps are there to the top of the Eiffel tower?

Answers

1. 1963
2. 237
3. 307 years
4. 163 km
5. 2,476
6. 248.5 years
7. M898
8. 38 minutes
9. 32
10. Ethiopia (95Million)
11. 30 days 12 hours and 30 minutes
12. 1 minute and 38 seconds
13. 9 minutes and 33 seconds
14. 1,642 metres or 5,387 feet
15. 80
16. 82,400,000 km2
17. 104,684
18. 1431
19. 350,710
20. 1st November 1956
21. 117
22. 627
23. 59
24. 1975
25. 1792

CPSIA information can be obtained
at www.ICGtesting.com
Printed in the USA
LVHW111737211119
638113LV00007B/1191/P